# TOMATO TIME!

by Albert Hinton

**PEARSON**

Glenview, Illinois • Boston, Massachusetts • Chandler, Arizona
Upper Saddle River, New Jersey

tomato

**Tomatoes Are Fruits**
    People often think that tomatoes are vegetables. But they are actually fruits!
    Tomatoes are juicy, like many fruits. But they are not as sweet.

**Healthful, But Messy**

Tomatoes are good for you! They have vitamins. Vitamins keep you healthy. They also help your body grow.

Try a tomato at snack time. Don't forget the napkins. Tomatoes can be messy!

**So Many Tomatoes!**

Tomatoes can be big or small. They can be red, green, yellow, or orange. Some even have stripes!

Different tomatoes have different names. Some have fun names like Lemon Boy and Big Tiger.

## How They Grow

Tomatoes grow on vines. The vine needs to be tied to sticks called stakes. Stakes help hold the heavy tomato vines up. That keeps the tomatoes off the ground.

**Grow Your Own!**

Tomatoes are easy to grow. Plant tomato seeds in the spring. Use good soil. Soon roots will begin to grow. Then the plant begins to come up out of the ground.

flower

ripe tomatoes

**Tips for Picking**

Little flowers grow on tomato plants. These flowers turn into tomatoes. Many tomatoes turn red when they are ripe. Don't pick the tomatoes until they're ripe and ready.

**Delicious!**

Some people put sliced tomatoes into salads. Some people like to cook tomatoes in pizza and other foods.

What is your favorite way to eat tomatoes?

## Talk About It

1. What colors can tomatoes be?
2. Why do tomato vines need to be tied to stakes?

## Write About It

3. This book tells you how a tomato plant grows. On a separate sheet of paper, draw a tomato plant. You can draw the roots, too! Use the pictures in this book to help you.

## Extend Language

Two parts of a plant are *roots* and *leaves*. Plant roots grow underground and take in water and food from the soil. Leaves grow on plant stems or branches. Which part gets more sunlight, the roots or leaves?

**Photographs Cover** ©Macdull Everton/Corbis; **1** ©Ariel Skelley/Corbis; **2** ©Macdull Everton/Corbis; **3** ©Ariel Skelley/Corbis; **4** ©David Prince/Corbis; **5** ©Patrick Johns/Corbis; **6** (TL) Getty Images, (TR) ©Jerome Wexler/Photo Researchers, Inc.; **7** (TL) ©George D. Lepp/Corbis, (TR) ©Royalty-Free/Corbis; **8** ©Michael Newman/PhotoEdit

| Genre | Build Background | Access Content | Extend Language |
|---|---|---|---|
| Nonfiction | • Plant Growth<br>• Tomatoes<br>• Gardening | • Labels in Pictures | • Plant Part Words |

**Scott Foresman Reading Street 2.4.2**

ISBN-13: 978-0-328-49655-6
ISBN-10: 0-328-49655-3